CATALYST RANCH

Where your vibe attracts your tribe

A Farm Animal Affirmation Coloring Journal
by Nicole B Roberts

This book belongs to

____

First edition published in the United States of America
August 2020
by
The Creative Catalyst LLC
www.TheCreativeCatalyst.Art

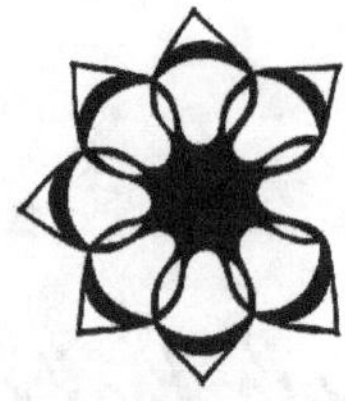

Dedicated to my maternal grandparents,
Rob & Arma Holman

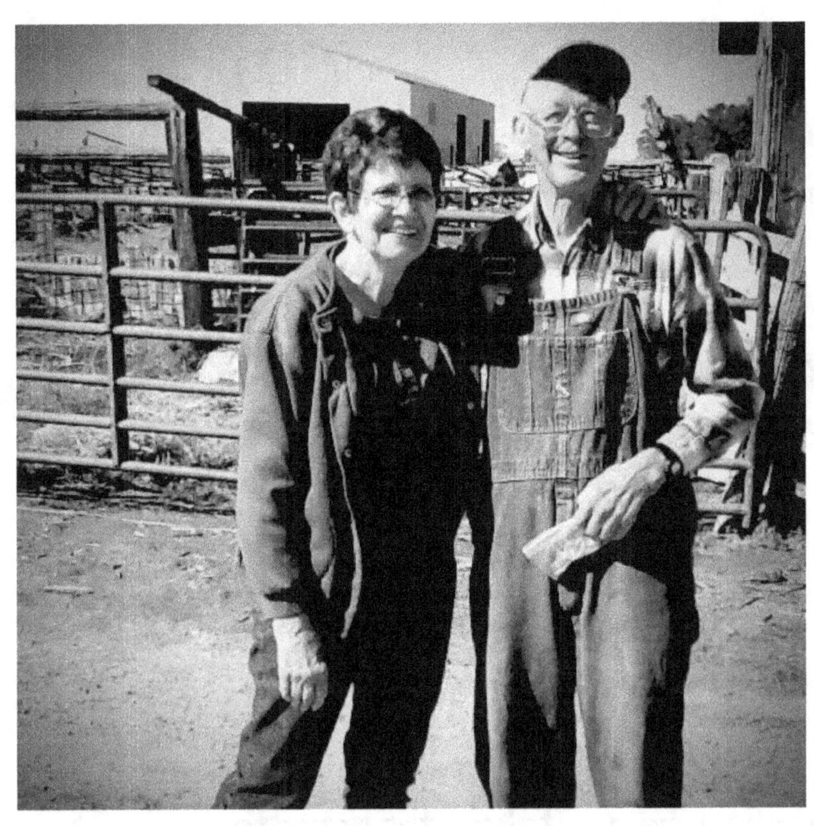

Their farm and small town way of life
was a bright spot in my childhood.
Their examples of hard work, positivity, service,
loyalty and love
are a heritage I bask in with pride and gratitude.
My simple hope is that I can perpetuate
a small part of their big legacy.

Introduction

Each animal in this book represents a positive
attribute that we can embody to improve the
quality of our lives.

When we meditate on the associated affirmation,
while physically creating a colorful symbol,
then express our thoughts through journaling,
we are more likely to integrate the attribute
into our lives.

When we display the symbol
and share our thoughts with others,
we become a catalyst that creates
even more ripples-
perpetuating positive change in ourselves
and attracting and growing our
"high vibe tribes".

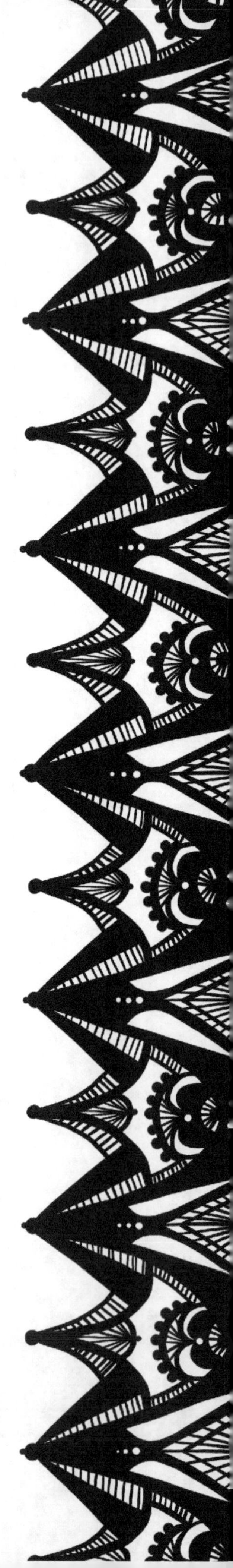

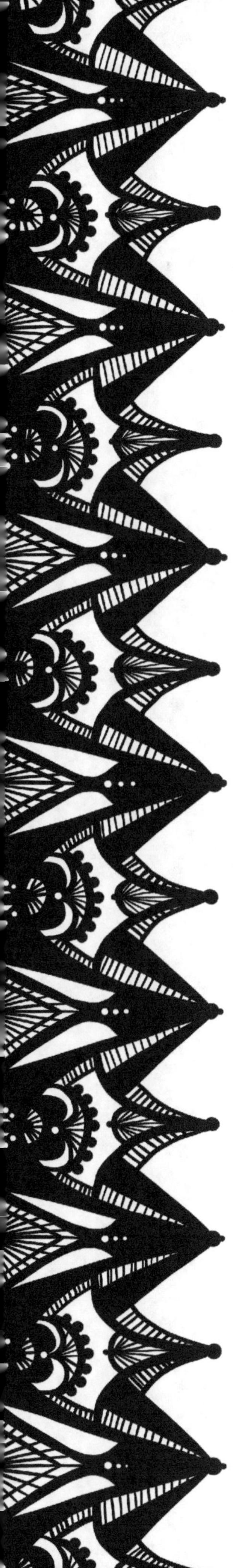

How to use this book

#1 On your own

Say the affirmation to yourself and contemplate
what it means as you color the picture.
Then, answer the prompt on the journal page.
Display your favorites where you can see them
as a reminder of the high vibe traits you possess.

#2 With your family or friends

Create a high vibe get-together.
Have each person pick which animal they are
drawn to, or put them face down and let people
pick at random.
Spend a few minutes doing the journal prompt.
Then, as you color your pictures, take turns
sharing your answers and discussing each
affirmation.
If you know each other well, take turns telling
other people how they embody the affirmation
they received.

For more ideas, visit:

TheCreativeCatalyst.Art

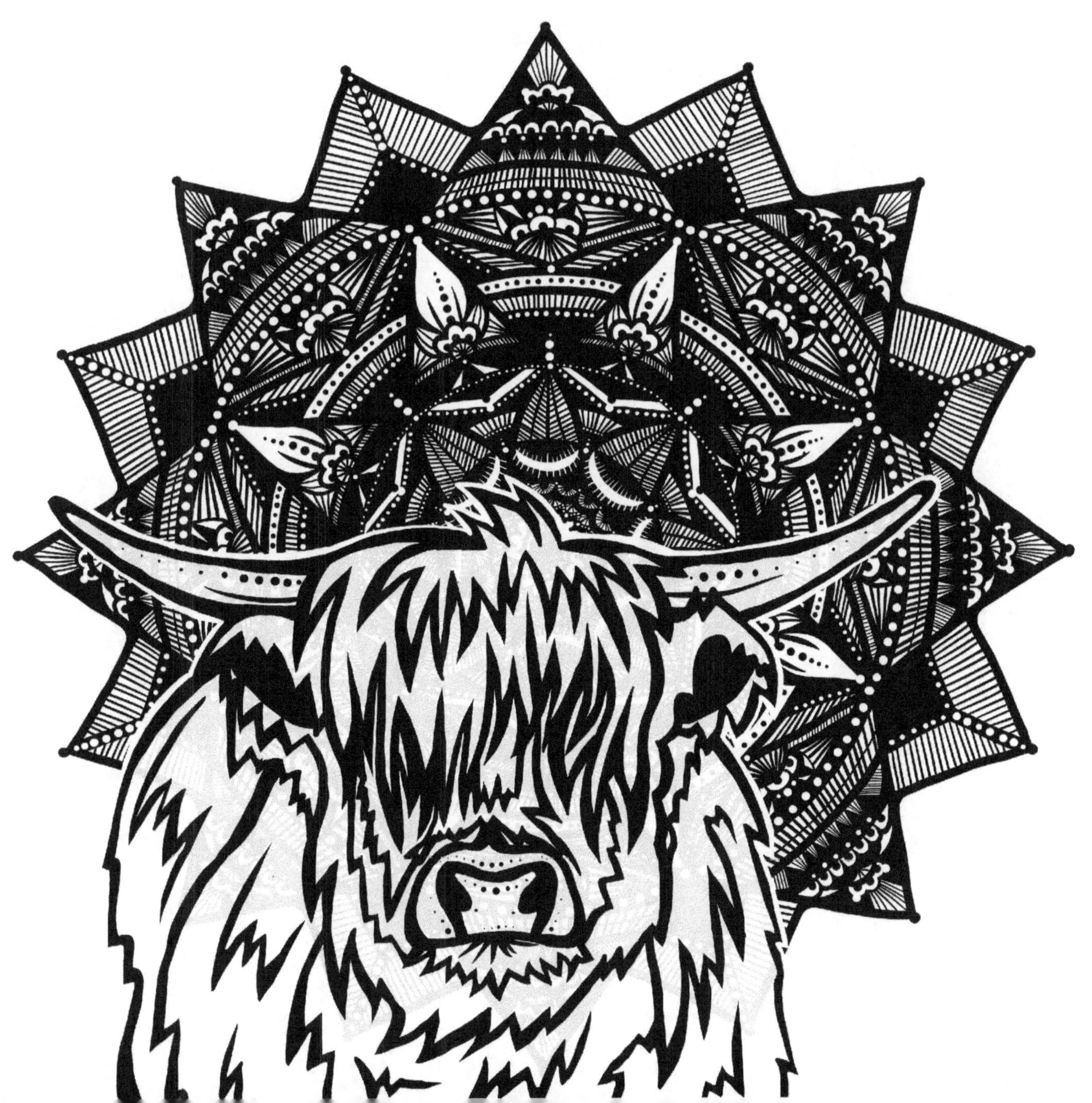
I am
RESILIENT

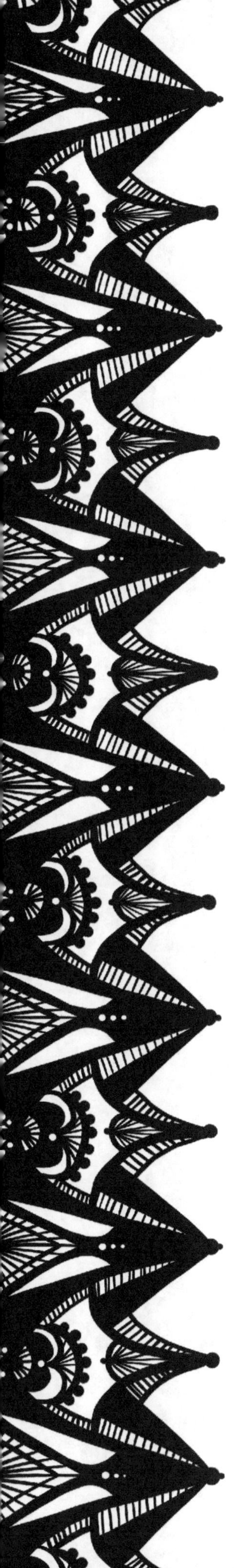

Consider a time you demonstrated this attribute.

**Consider how this attribute improves the
quality of your life.**

I am
GENTLE

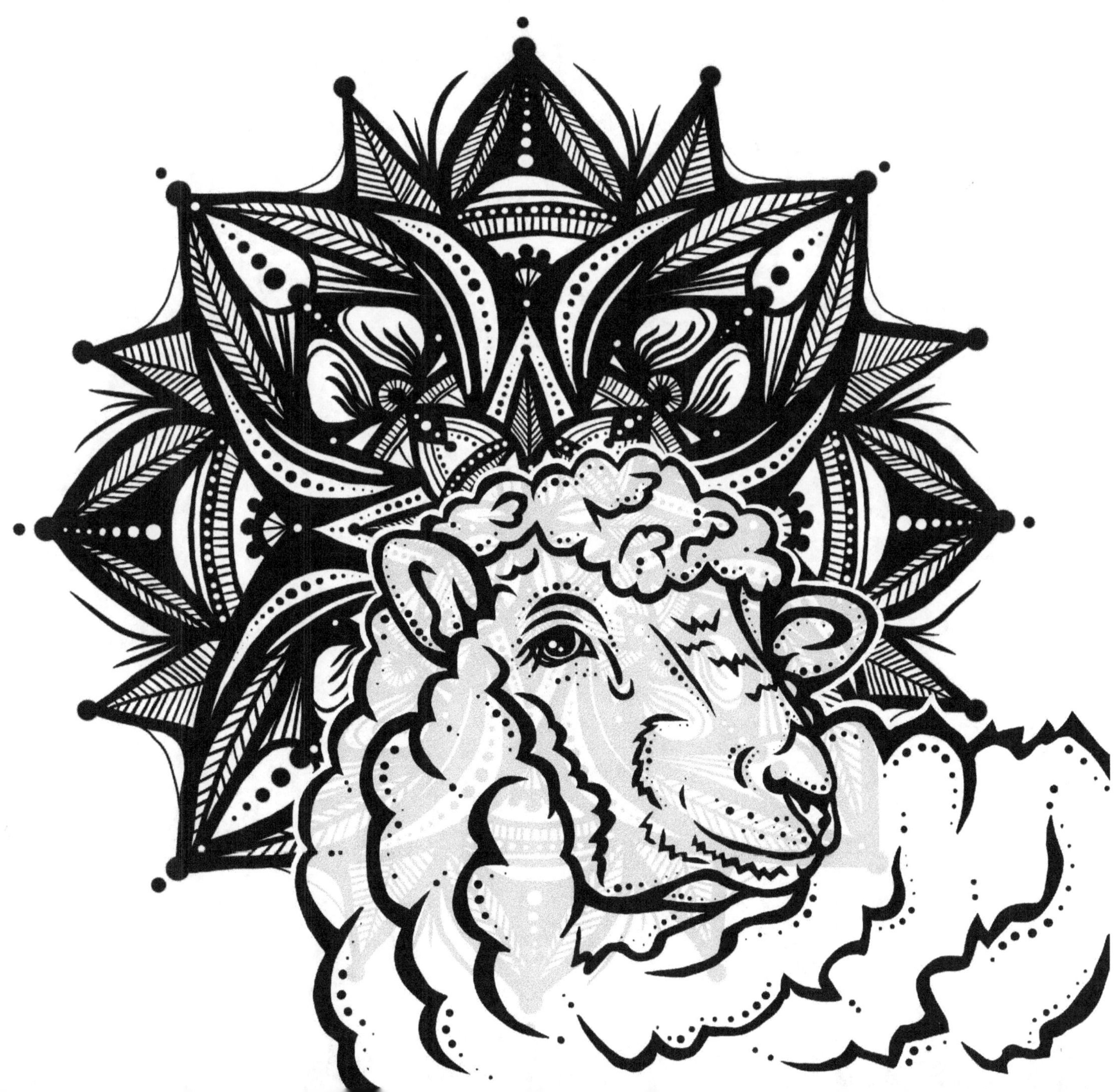

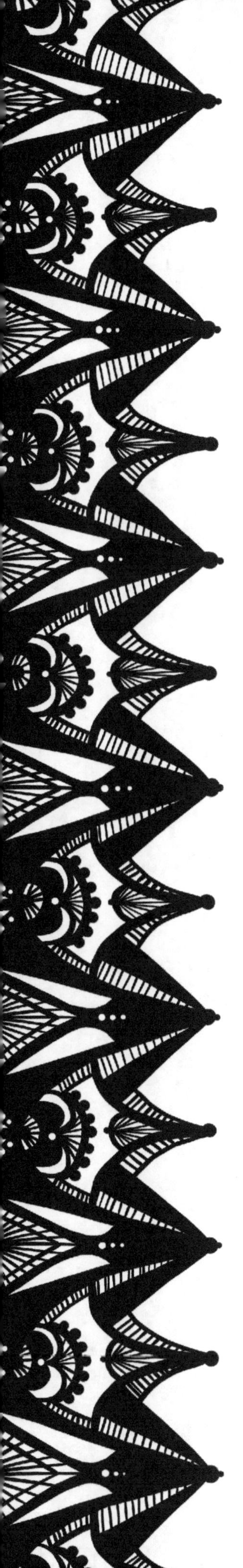

Consider a time you demonstrated this attribute.

Consider how this attribute improves the
quality of your life.

I am
CREATIVE

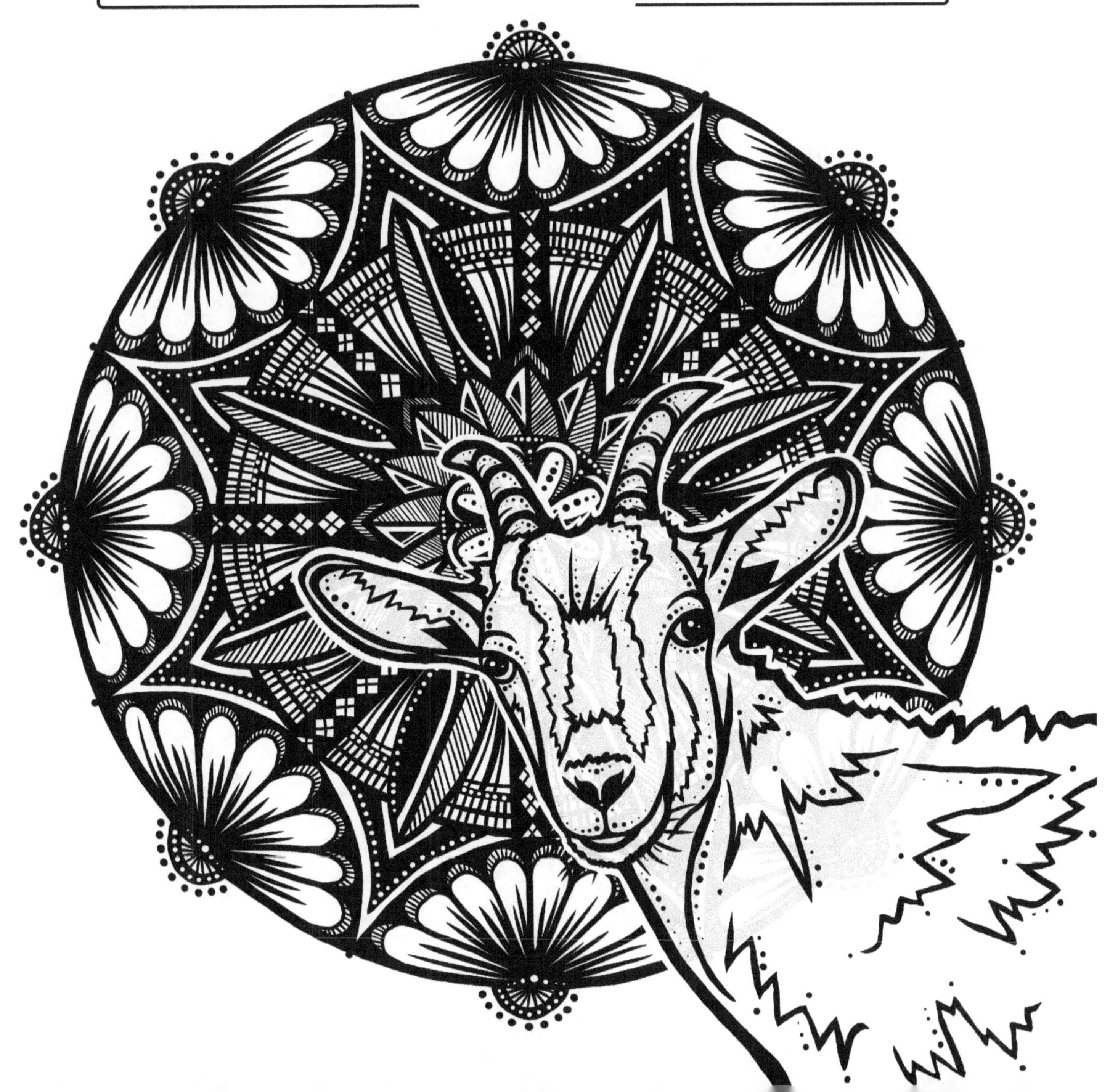

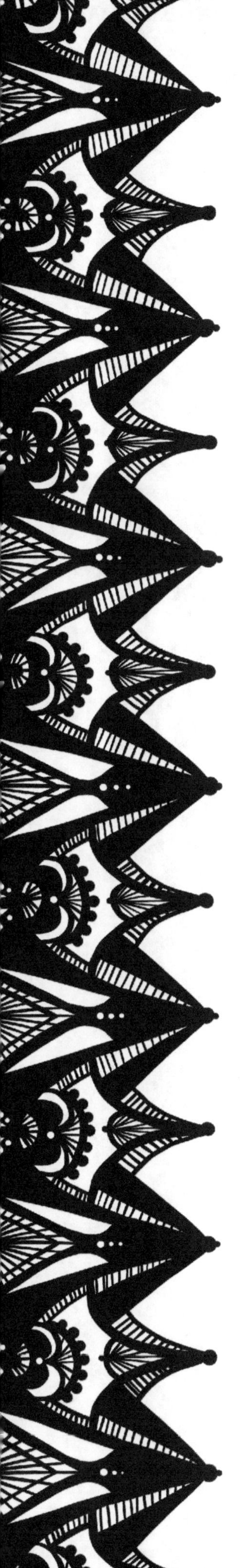

Consider a time you demonstrated this attribute.

Consider how this attribute improves the
quality of your life.

I am
CURIOUS

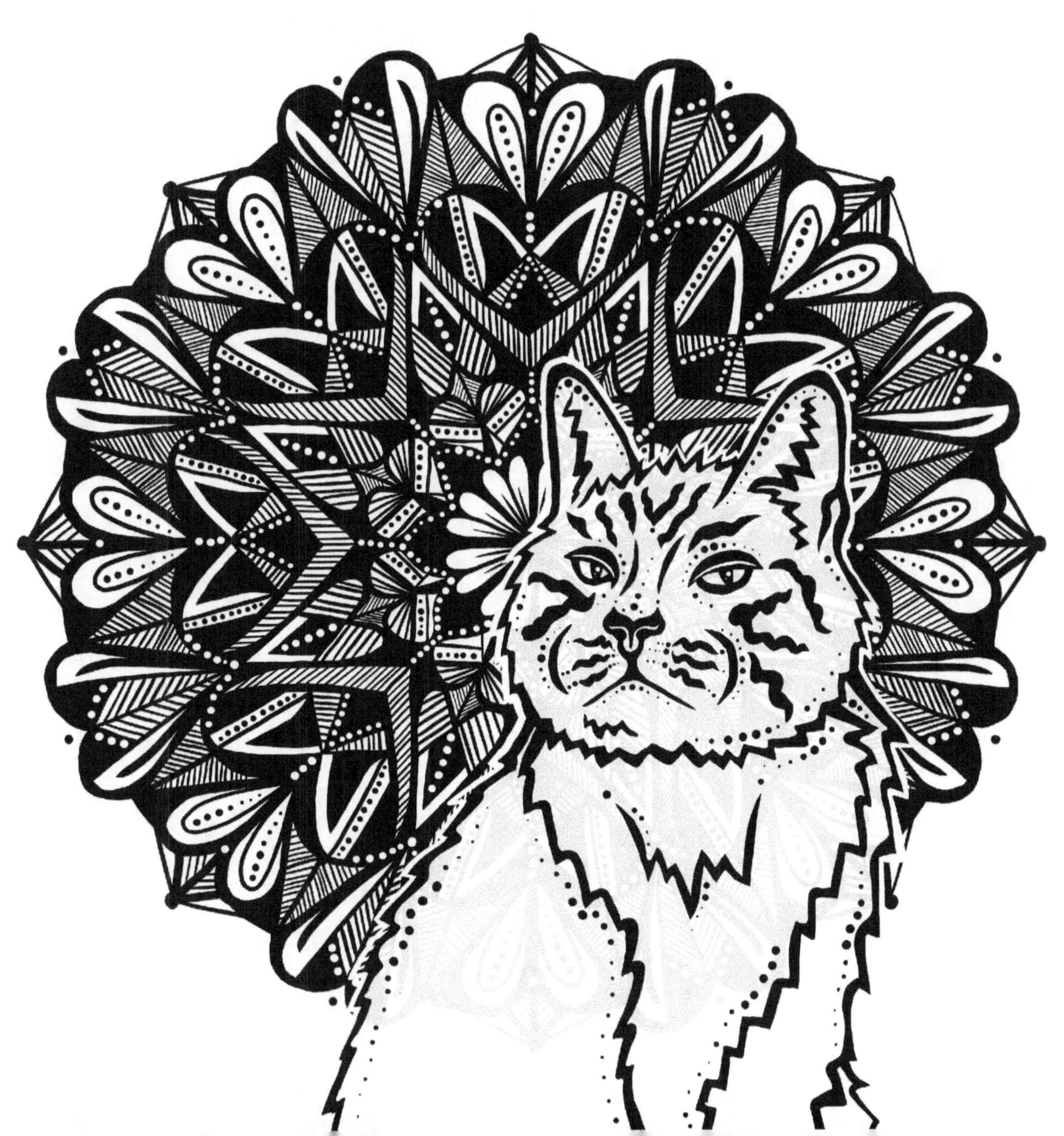

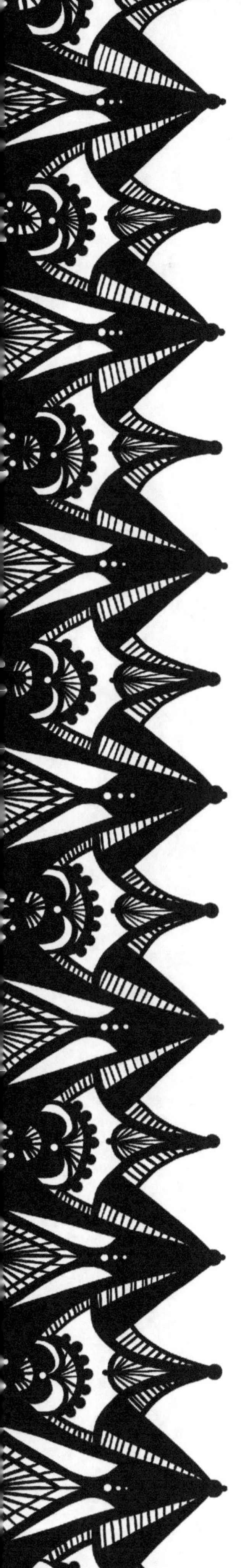

> *"Nothing in life is to be feared, it is only to be understood.*
> *Now is the time to understand more,*
> *so that we may fear less."*
> Marie Curie

Consider a time you demonstrated this attribute.

Consider how this attribute improves the quality of your life.

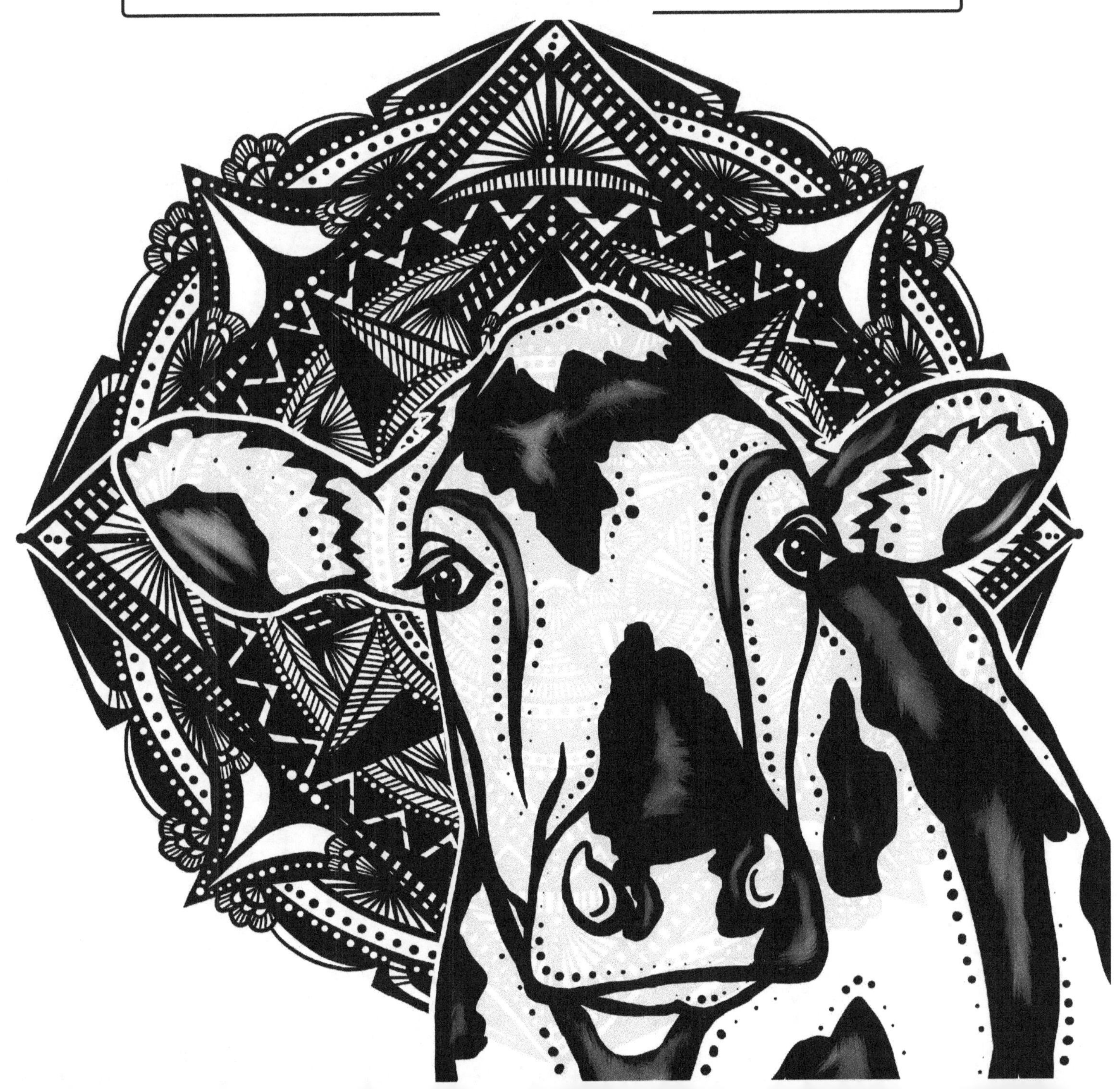

I am
NURTURING

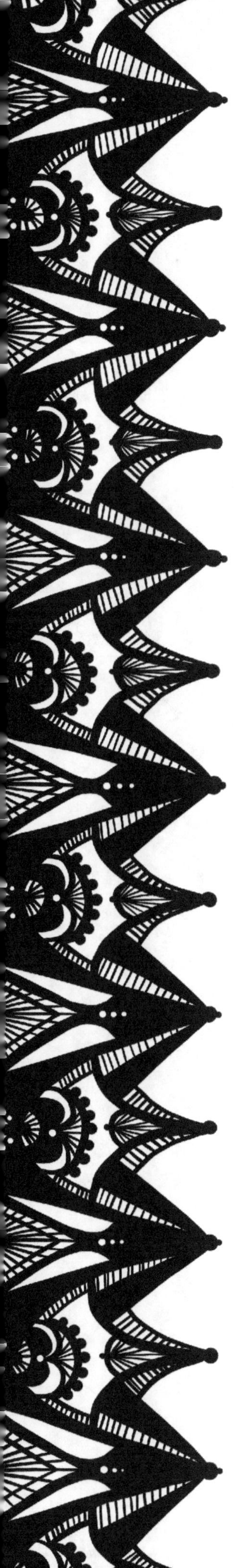

Consider a time you demonstrated this attribute.

Consider how this attribute improves the quality of your life.

I am
ABUNDANT

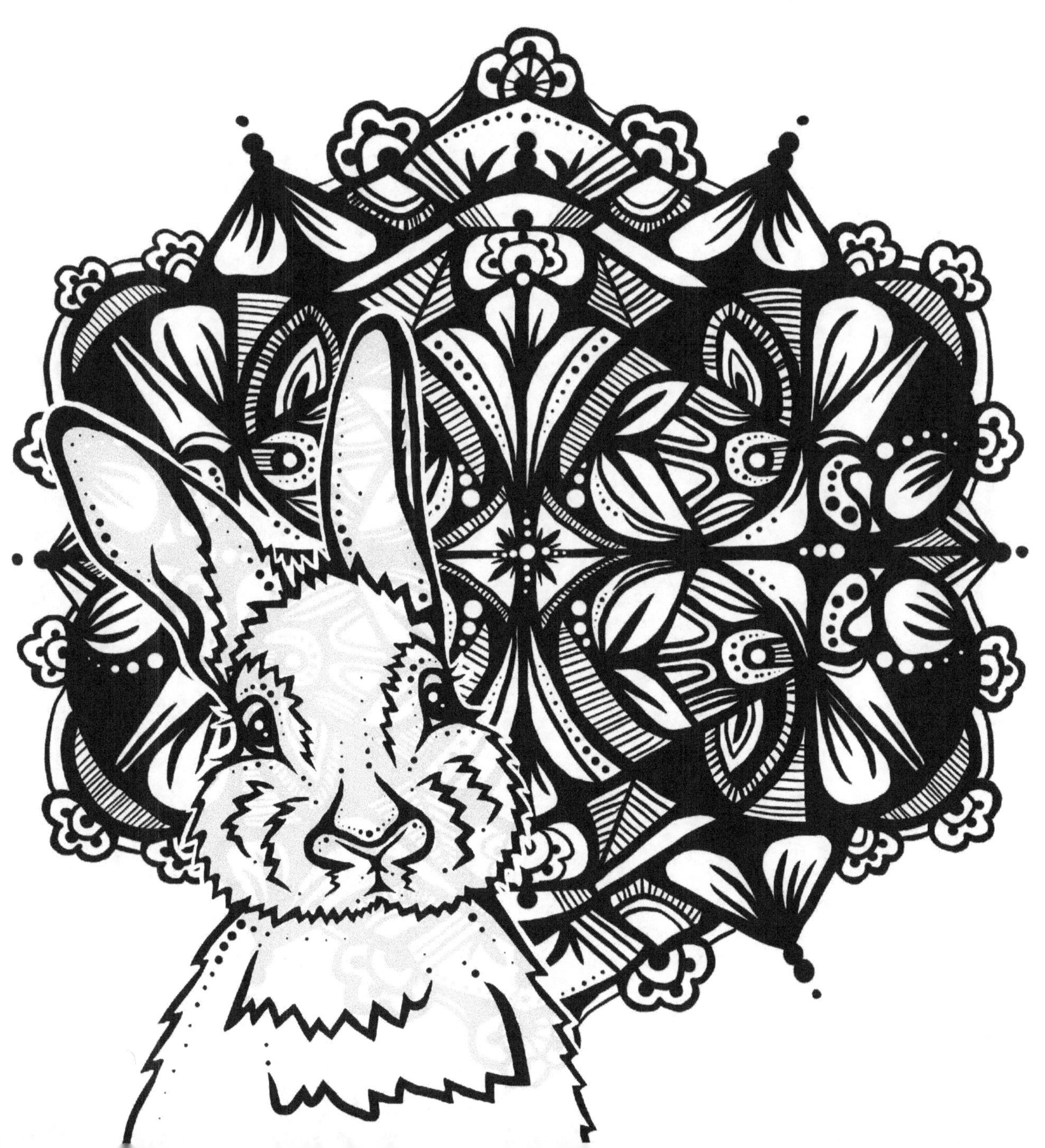

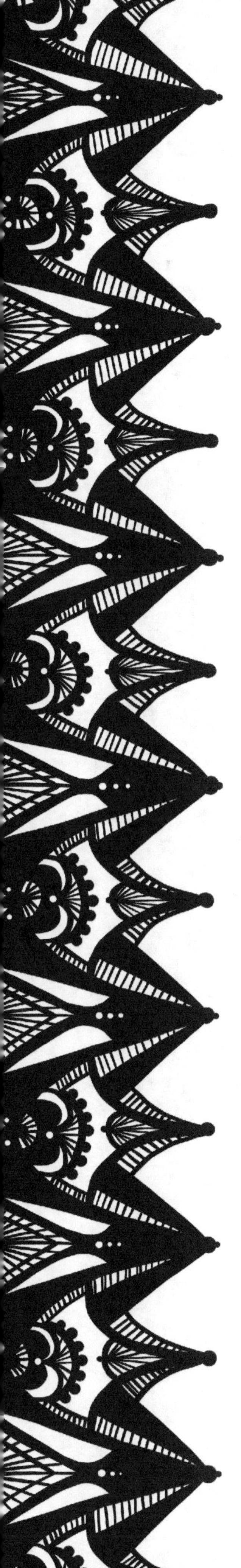

Consider a time you demonstrated this attribute.

Consider how this attribute improves the
quality of your life.

I am
JUBILANT

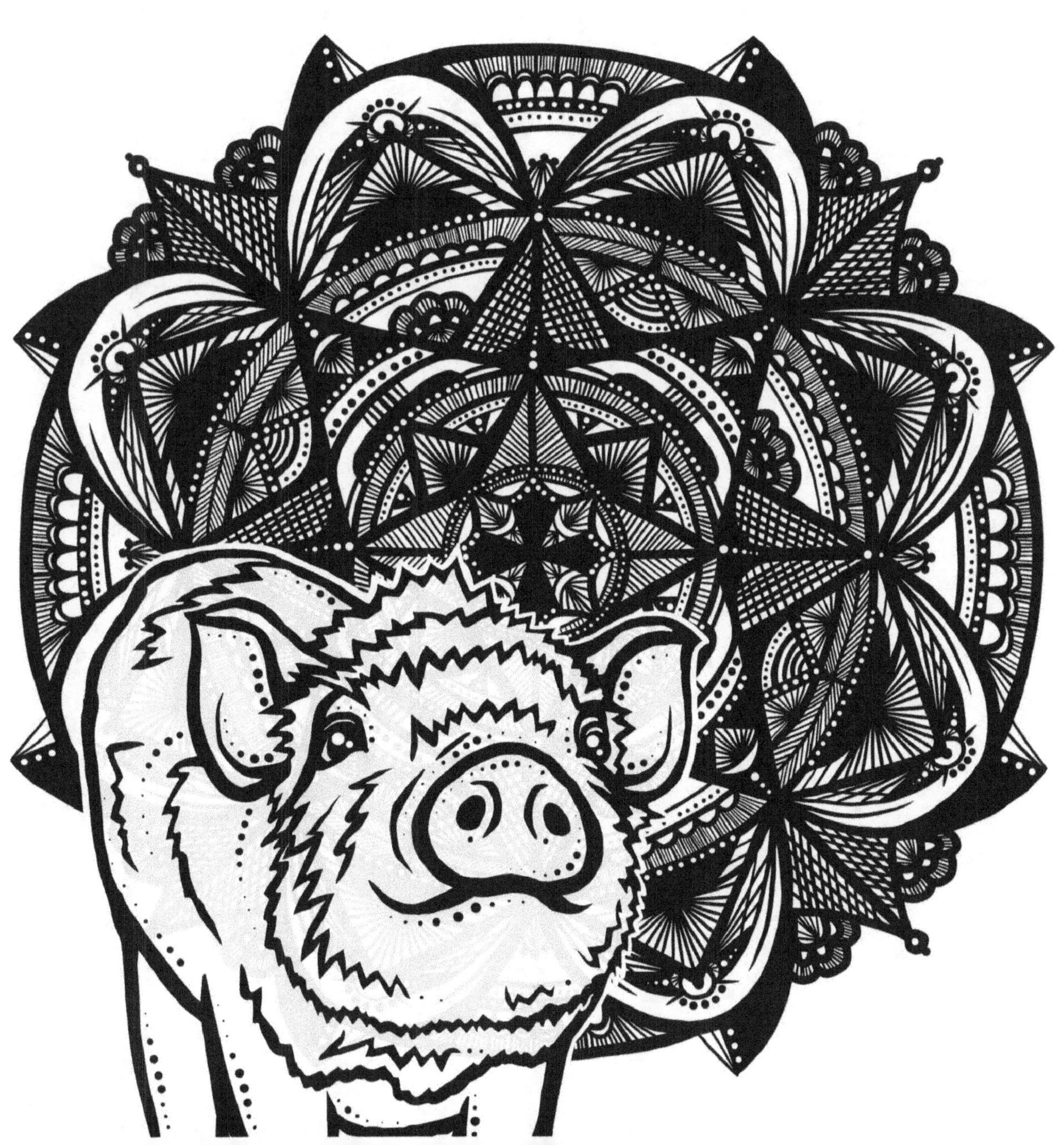

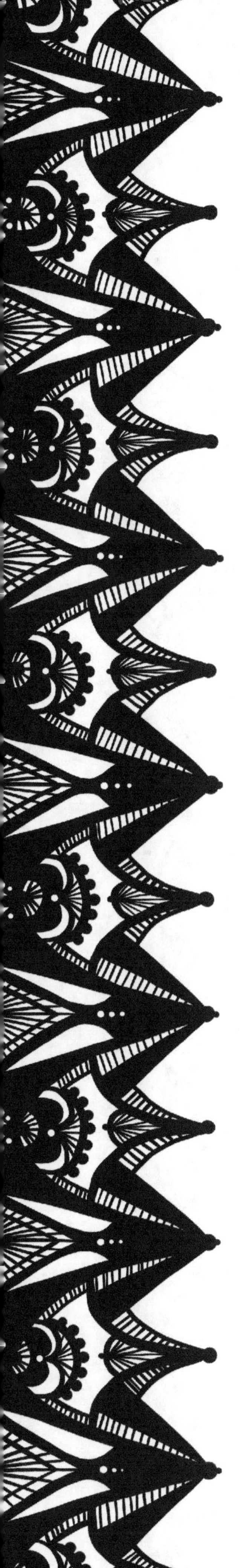

Consider a time you demonstrated this attribute.

**Consider how this attribute improves the
quality of your life.**

I am
CONFIDENT

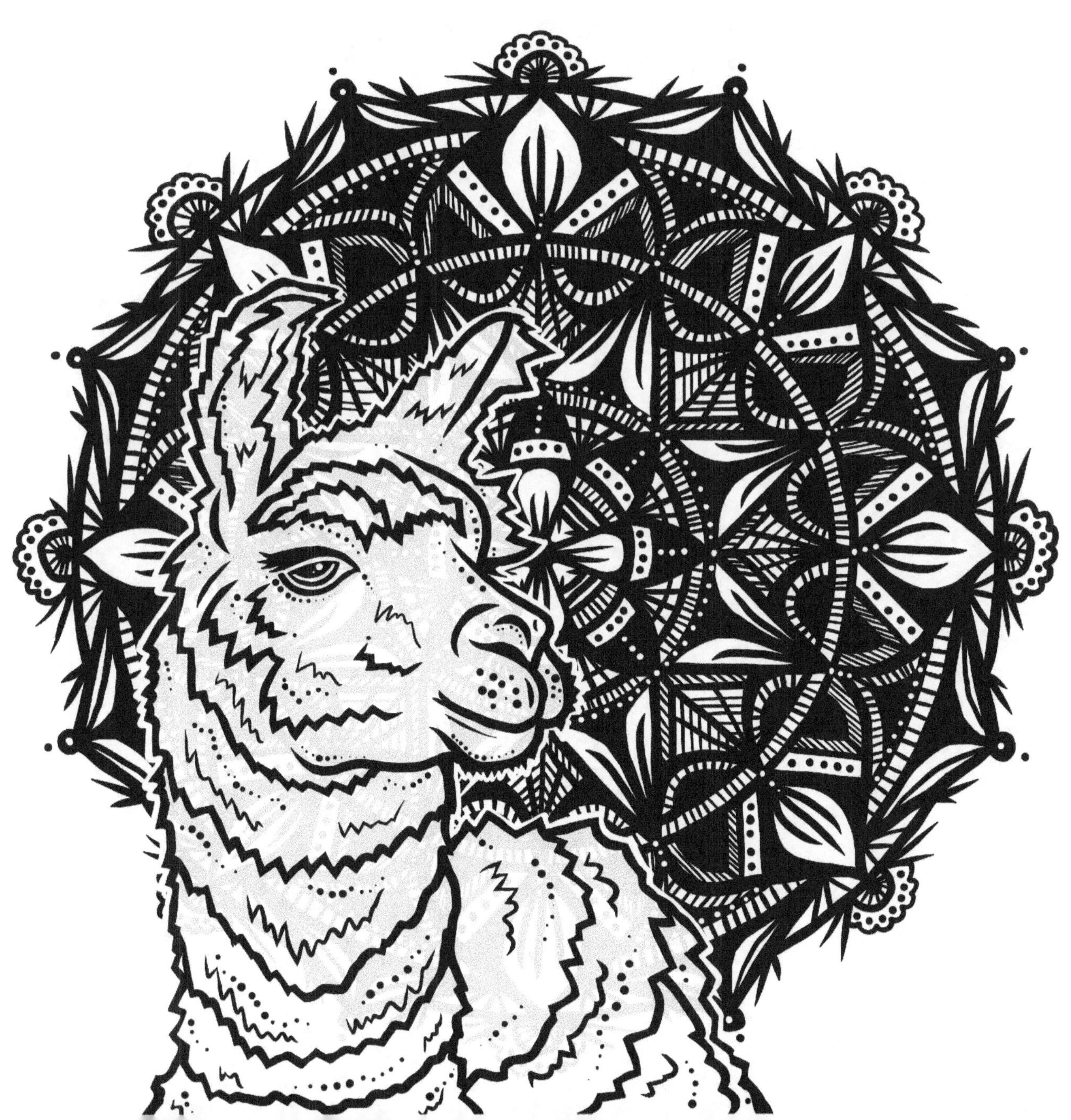

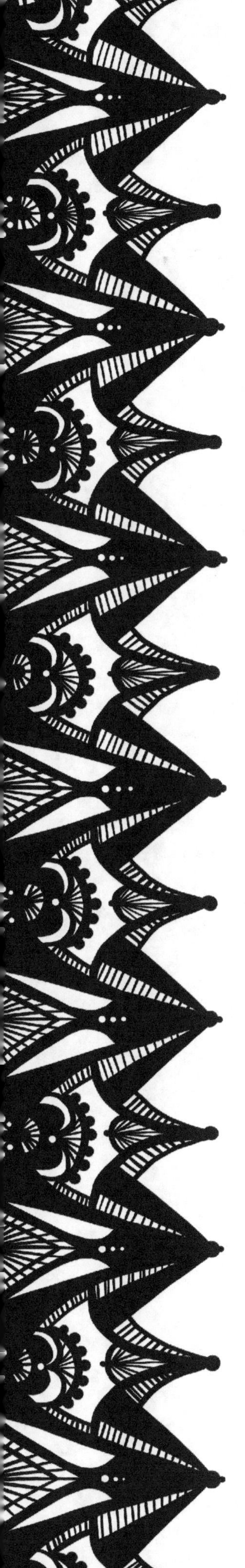

> "Just be yourself. Let people see the real, imperfect, flawed, quirky, weird, beautiful and magical person that you are."
> Mandy Hale

Consider a time you demonstrated this attribute.

Consider how this attribute improves the quality of your life.

I am
EXPRESSIVE

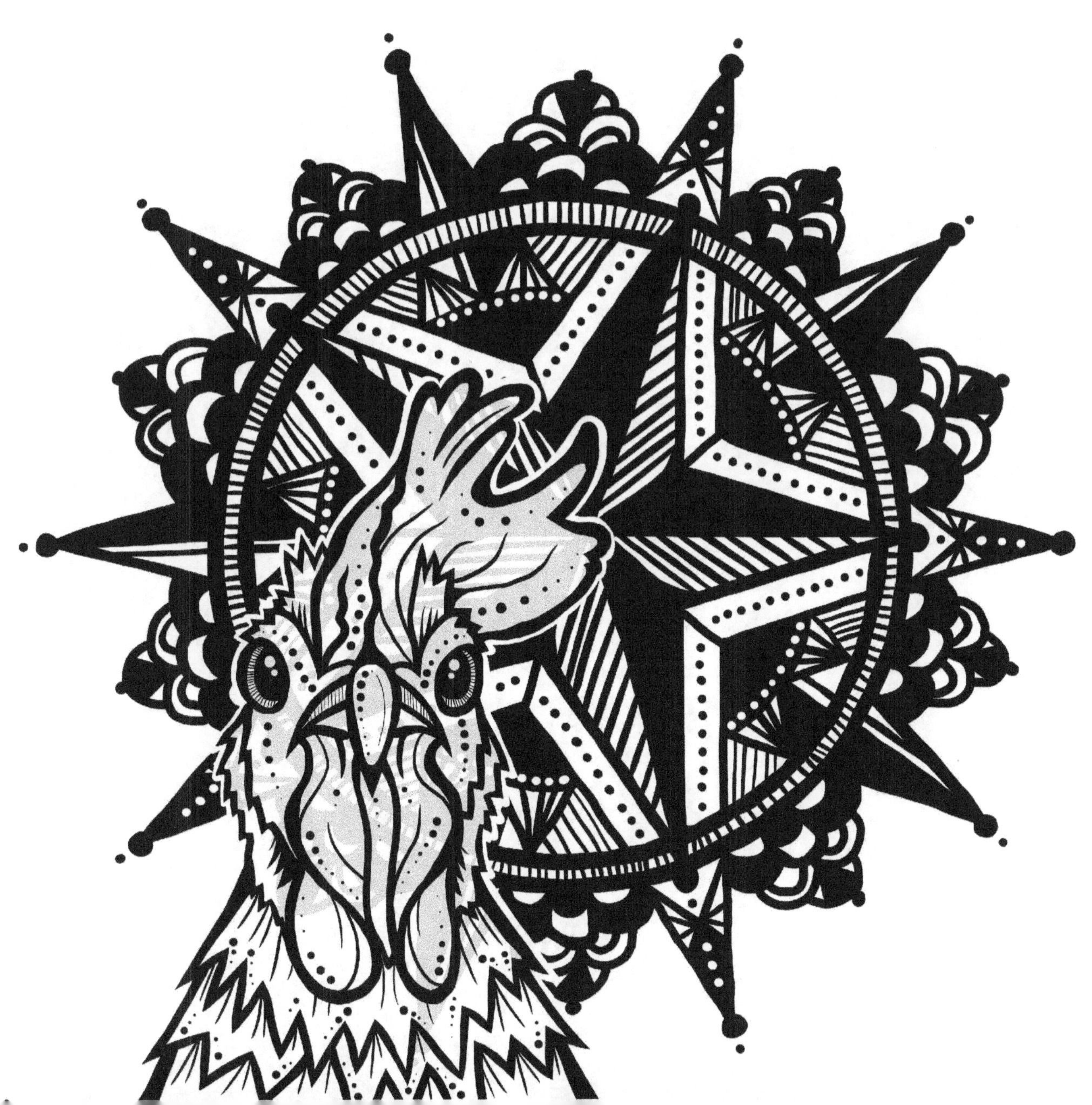

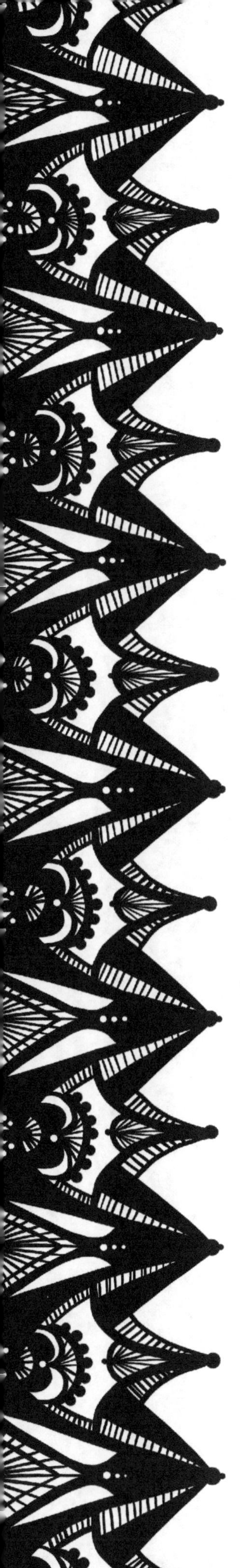

Consider a time you demonstrated this attribute.

**Consider how this attribute improves the
quality of your life.**

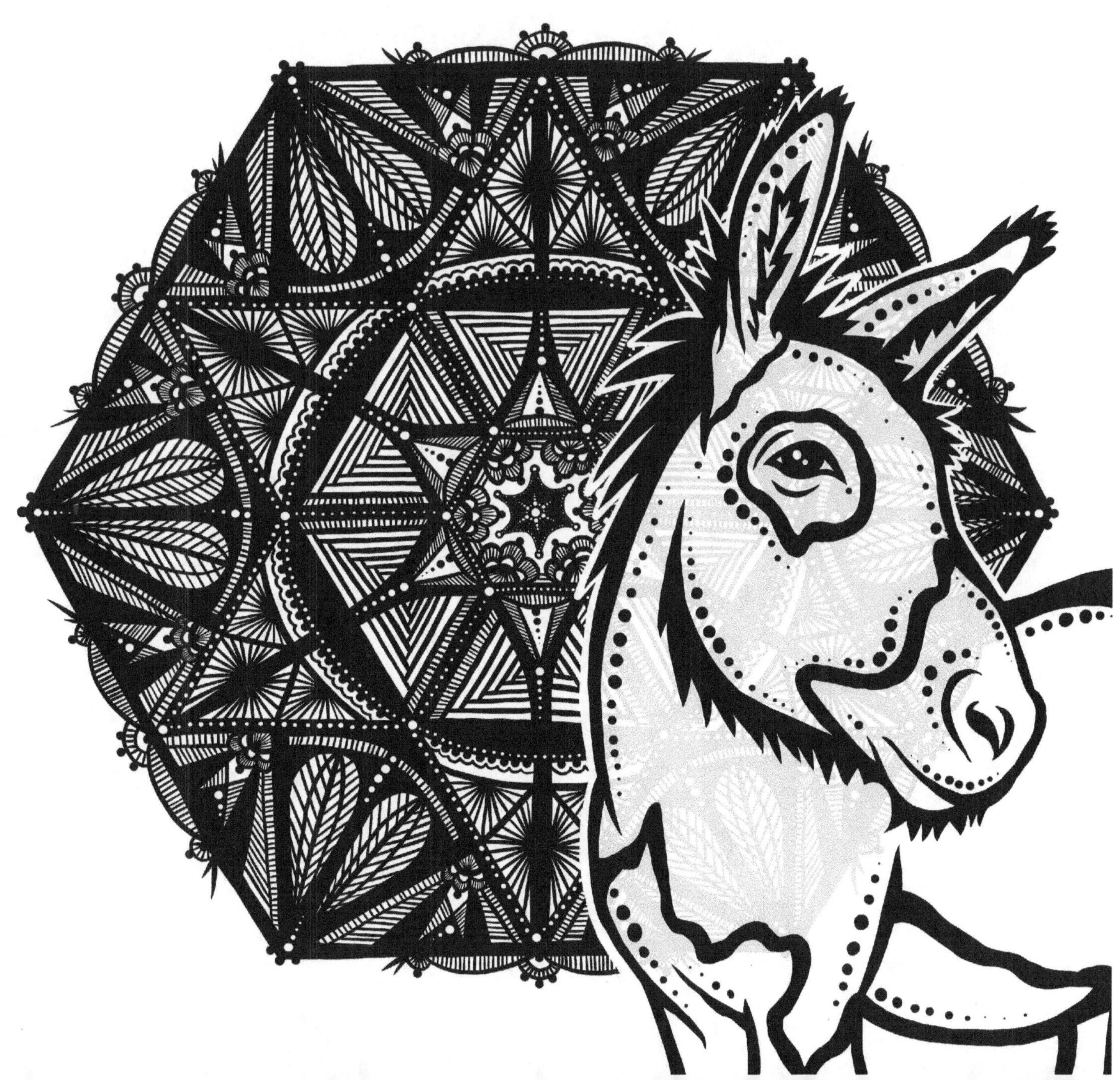
I am
PERSISTENT

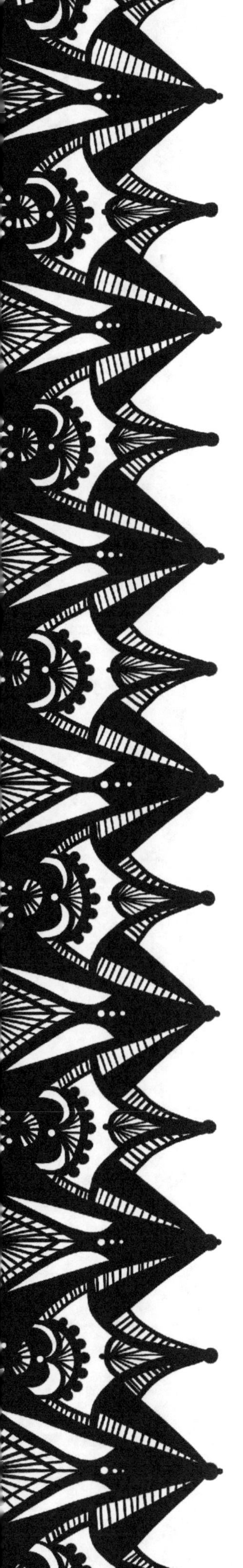

Consider a time you demonstrated this attribute.

Consider how this attribute improves the
quality of your life.

I am
ENERGETIC

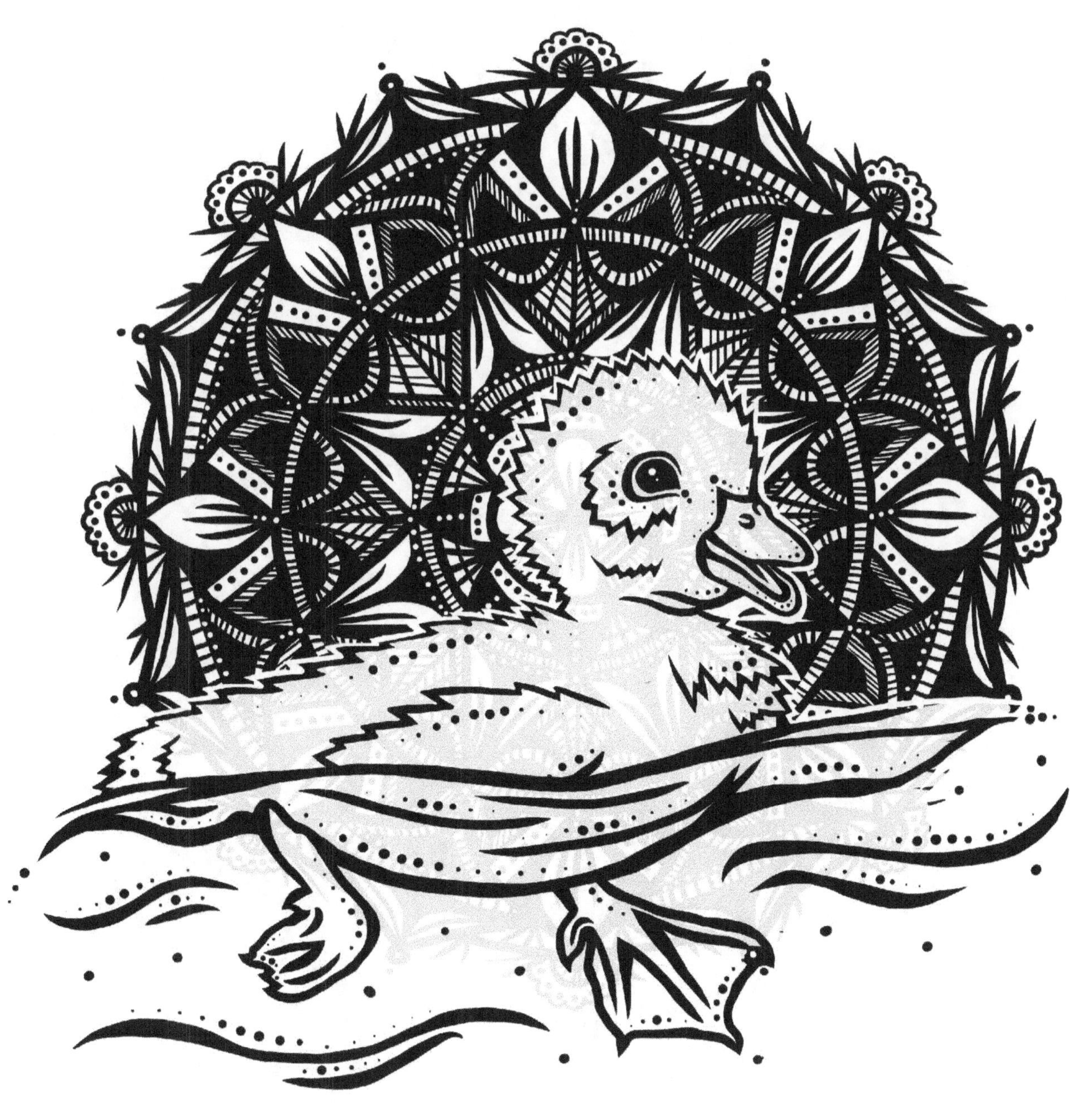

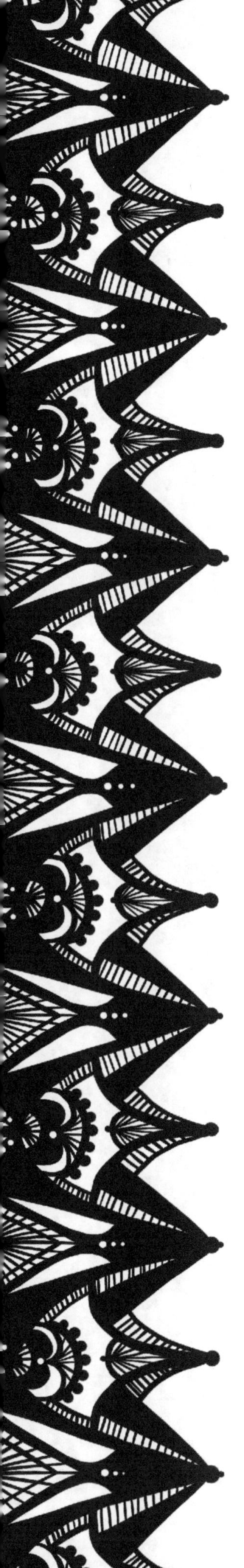

*"Nothing great was ever achieved
without enthusiasm."*
Ralph Waldo Emerson

Consider a time you demonstrated this attribute.

**Consider how this attribute improves the
quality of your life.**

I am
CONTENT

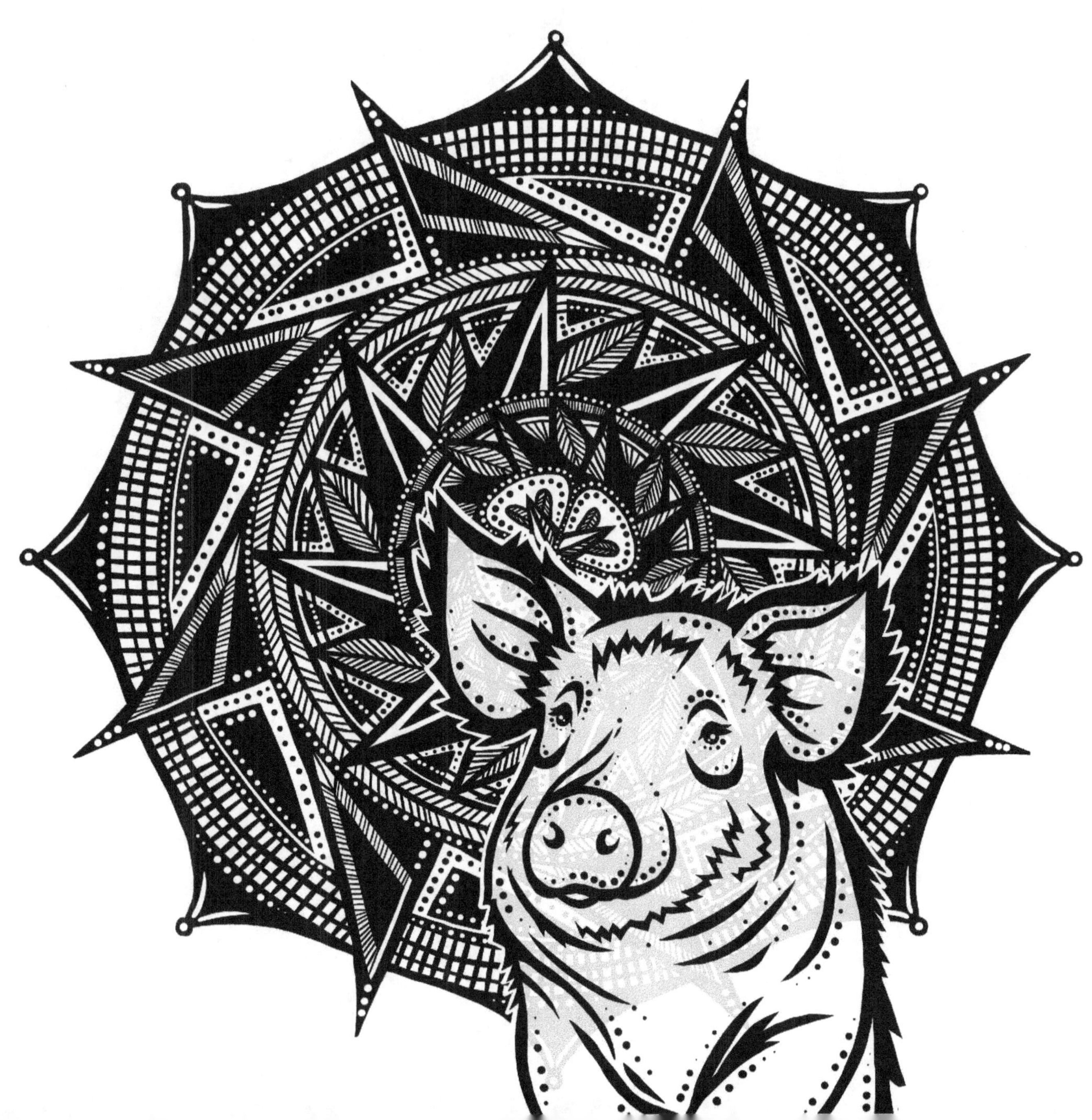

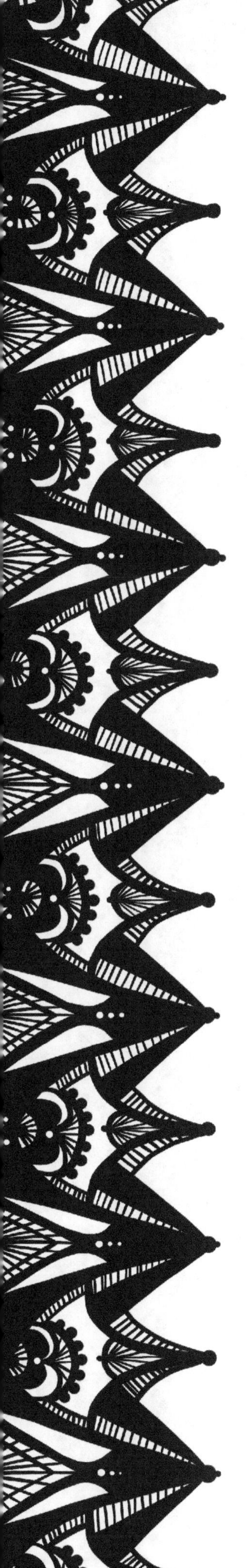

Consider a time you demonstrated this attribute.

**Consider how this attribute improves the
quality of your life.**

About the Creator

Nicole B Roberts

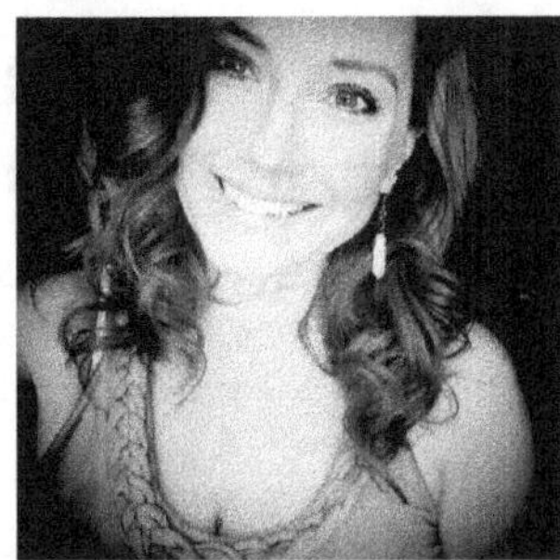

is a self-taught artist, an author,
and a free-spirited creator
attempting to gracefully raise three wild offspring
while chasing her bearded husband
on his oilfield adventures in Midland, TX.

Raised beneath the mountains in West Jordan, UT by
an outdoorsman/ book salesman and an artist/
elementary school teacher likely sparked her lifelong
love of learning.

She is ever inspired by nature, color, cycles,
symbolism, growth, finding the good in people,
authenticity, vulnerability, the magic of words
and above all, love.

Her purpose in all she does is to model and reiterate
that we were each "created to create"
and that our joy is hiding within
the acceptance of that divine identity.

You can see which creative squirrels she is chasing
next at:

TheCreativeCatalyst.Art

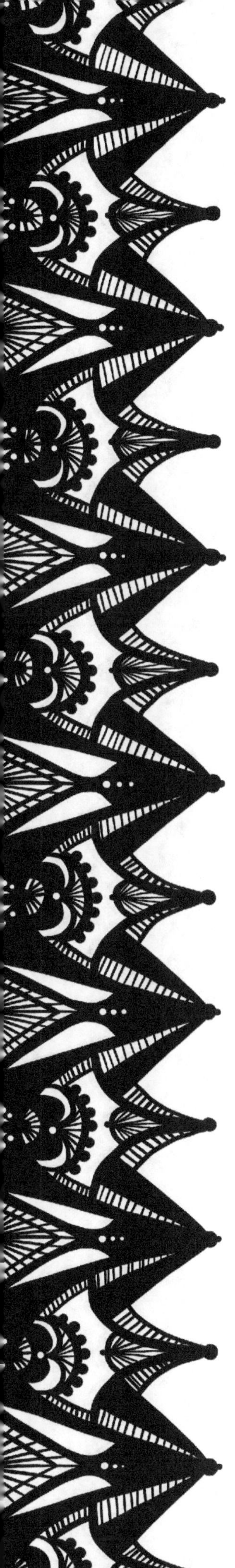

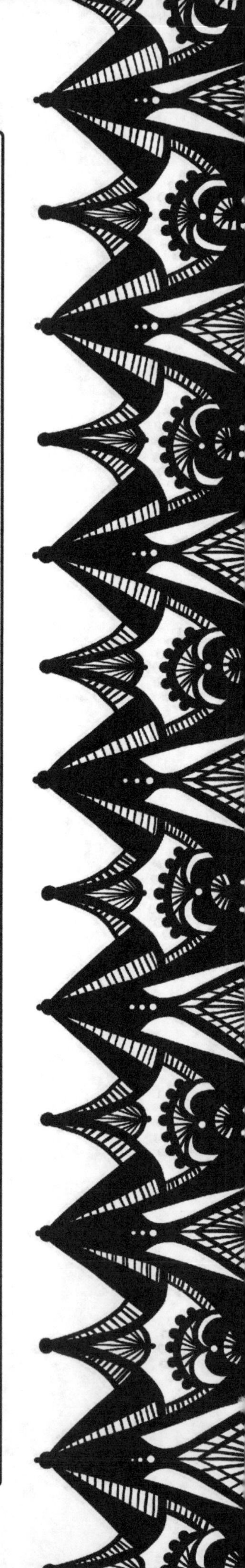

www.ingramcontent.com/pod-product-compliance
Lightning Source LLC
Chambersburg PA
CBHW082246060726

47598CB00017B/2852